All rights reserved.

ISBN: 9781793492876

DEDICATION

For all you devoted your life in living for the Lord Jesus and believing that is our God; grace and dignity will be rendered against you; As you read this book, be happy in the knowledge you have, to believe that Jesus Christ, hath redeemed us from the curse of this world which is poverty terms.

" This Book dedicated to be yours, in all peace brings comfort to each other, if one can believe it; really saved or not but either believes in Him that is your Creator, you can identify that, being poor is a disgrace; is a personal embarrassment and do not inspire comfort to communities and to the National in holistic, because the promise of a hundred times yet still make for you, will you do so that you can see that hundred in your life. now it is the opportunity to read this book to archive these goals. However this book is for you; targeted to give you knowledge; I'm sure after receive it; you will never remain as poor again.

DIE POOR!? Yes/no!!

CONTENTS

Dedication……………………………….

Acknowledgments… ……… VII

Chapter one …………………………2

Chapter two………………… ……12

Chapter three……………………….23

Chapter four …………………….33

Chapter five……………………….. 52

Chapter six……………… ……….64

ACKNOWLEDGMENTS.

This book is the result of a research of poverty for a long time I made, the research comes from myself for being poor for several time, without having to get rid of income to satisfy my needs and my family too. It's like this book lies in my heart since long time. Broadly personally I hate POVERTY AS I HATE HELL.

Being poor is a shame and disgrace for a man who recognize himself that he has saved or has sane and calls Jesus Christ is Lord and Savior of his life.

Thanks .

CHAPTER ONE : WHATS POVERTY

Poverty to me means going without the basic means to live happily. I don't think the term poverty is limited to a lack material resources such as money, a home, food and so on that make you poor, it could include limited access to education, or employment services. Whatever in their life that I lacking, a person living in poverty is reduced to feeling inferior, inadequate, and unhappy. If poor health, domestic violence, abuse, bad nutrition, inadequate housing and lack of opportunity are the symptoms, poverty is often the cause.

To me poverty is more than just a low household income. Poverty is a mind-set, a way of thinking that is self-deprecating and self-fulfilling. Poverty is often quiet to those who don't face it, but loud to those who do. In this sense poverty is actually relative. Other country does not have the same poverty as the third world, I

have seen that with my own eyes. This means in equal access to opportunities and creates unhappiness and feeling of deprivation. Lack of income aside, to me poverty is a FEELING that people have, caused often by their own sense of hopelessness that their situation can ever improve. True poverty in my mind, exists on many levels. It's not necessarily the lack of money, rather, the imposition of barriers. Barriers to healthcare, barriers to education, barriers to choice.

True poverty imposes a burden on its bearer to perpetuate patterns that binds the next generation to the same cycle insomuch that the cycle becomes clear. At that point when these ideas are embedded in a society, true poverty exists. This means that the individual is no longer deprived of choice, but deprived of thought, hope and imagination that any possibility exists outside of what they've inherited. I believe poverty is defined as an area where you are held back because of a "lack of." This could include clothing, money, education or housing. I believe that poverty

and development are closely interlinked and that the thing that hinders development for all individuals is the constraints that are put in place to restrict ones freedom. I believe that poverty is something that can be changed and it unfortunately places lives on an unequal footing to others.

Poverty can put lives at risk and is something that desperately needs to be changed. Poverty is about low living standards and is often measured in terms of income. However poverty extends beyond income to include factors such as health and education. Normally poverty is classified within two categories: absolute and relative. Absolute poverty refers to a set standard across countries while relative poverty refers to people being poor relative to those around them. Poverty to me is not a lack of funds but a lack in hope, aspirations and drive. It's a state of mind or perception. I personally know a huge number of people that live 'below the standard' but the perception of capability and potential to do great things differs. I see

intergenerational cycles of beneficiary dependency, unemployment and worst of all no aspiration to move away from this lifestyle. This to me is poverty. When you say poverty – the first thing that comes to mind is Africa. In other countries especially those educated, I feel it is underprivileged or disadvantage families or individuals who lack the ability to deal with life's everyday trials.

Temptations like alcohol and drugs help these families to cope with life, although the effects are devastating. I feel underprivileged it is not being able to provide the basic necessities. Instead of cooked meals - its cheap food from the takeaways. Instead of sending the kids to school with no lunch -it's no school until payday. Instead of dealing with health issues -it will have to wait until we have gas to go to the doctors. Instead of saving money to buy what you really need - you get a loan from a family member or ring the money shop or the home direct truck or take something into the pawn shop to trade for money.

Some effects of drugs and alcohol is violence, abuse, self-doubt and an inability to interact with society. Children's health, education and financial stability are at risk. It is a generational cycle and it will not stop until someone finds a different path – explores or steps outside of what they are used to. Children will only learn from what they see. Poverty is an affliction that lies largely outside of the hands of those afflicted, unless they create or are given the tools which with to tackle it. It is lack of access to basic necessities, it is the root of the deepest and darkest problems in society, and it is entirely unnecessary and absolutely changeable.

"Poverty" to me is a socially constructed and unnecessary state of being that is used to keep power imbalances in place. It may be a negative opinion but it is my belief that improving benefits and the minimum wage would heavily diminish poverty in many countries if not eradicate it completely. Poverty is hunger, isolation, disempowerment and uncertainty.

Poverty does not exist in a bubble and is so often the precursor to many other social problems such as mental illness, crime and poor education. Poverty is deprivation, including of opportunity It is often (but not only) acute, where a person is deprived of necessities eg. food, shelter, and basic social connection) crucial for simple survival. When a person is deprived of necessities, it is hard to maintain psychological grit and physical health or care about the good things in life. Disconnection limits the ability for a person to achieve their goals—worse, sometimes it limits the desire to set goals. Where deprivation is of non-essentials, it is still possible to experience 'poverty of opportunity'.

Poverty is not acceptable anywhere, least of all in all country. Poverty represents the extreme of inequity in society. It is a multifaceted issue that places its sufferers at a disadvantage in every aspect of their life, development and career. It is not simply about a lack of money, but describes the cumulative effect that a lack

of the basic necessities has on a person over an extended period of time, negatively influencing health, mental development, social and economic security and creating a barrier of negative societal perception and low self-esteem that prevents people leaving the poverty cycle. Poverty is a lack of choice. Whether it be through not being able to feed your children or through ending up in a life of crime due to society expecting it.

This is why I strive to empower those vulnerable groups to give them a voice and ultimately to give them choice over how they live their lives. Examples range from foster kids regardless of background being automatically labeled as delinquents to poorer communities being marginalized outside of the main economic hubs and unable to find work as a result. I have to admit I come from privileged beginnings, I don't ever remember seeing poverty or being aware enough to notice it where I grew up. I may have been told, I may have been given data and stats and numbers. None of this computed until I saw it face to face.

I want to tell the truth that poverty is going without. It's facing needs that you are unable to meet yourself and your community is unable to help with. It's not having the freedom to choose another option for your life because you are without the very things you need to get by. Growing up within a middle class working family however growing up within a poverty stricken area i was able to see poverty full frontal from the young age of three. Poverty is not all about not having money, it's about not having the necessities to live, being unhappy and having constant worry. Poverty is about not having clean clothes on your back and breakfast on the table every morning. We can discuss relative and complete poverty however once you're in poverty it is hard to differentiate. Poverty is about having the happiness taken away, it is about waking up in the morning worrying that today my children won't be fed and today I have to worry about how I'm going to pay all the bills stacking up.

Poverty is social segregation it is not a happy place

and it needs to be changed by us. As Nelson Mandela said;

"Like slavery and apartheid poverty is not natural. It is manmade and it can be overcome and eradicated by the actions of human beings".

An interpretation that I sympathized with is that it is a restriction put on individuals or groups whereby it unfairly limits human potential. In my opinion, 'unfairly' does not necessarily mean that there is no way out of poverty, it just means that the determinants are so stacked against the individual or group that there is little chance to live a fulfilling life. The limits are often described in terms of a monetary value, however I believe it has the potential to be extended beyond that to environmental and societal factors for example. There is also an element of relativity to this which is weighed up against the society in which it exists - e.g. poverty in AFRICA.

DIE POOR!? Yes/no!!

THE CHAPTER TWO.

Speech analysis and fact.

Broadly I was touched by the message of the President of the United States denigrate Donald Trump for blacks. Here I will give a few quotes.

"If God wanted to create same whites and blacks and the Arabs would have made us equally uniform color and minds. But he created us differently. White, black, yellow,... Mentally whites have more ability than blacks and Arabs. That attested without doubt for many years now. I believe the white man is an honest man, faithful, with the fear of God, and who can show actions the real meaning of being human. Blacks and Arabs nothing they think more than shouting, love, music, polygamy, alcohol, superstition, sex nasty, pretending they'd worship, jealousy, strife,

and complained of poor leadership, but do not take any action to eliminate the bad administration office. Weeping just yet, and in case the get opportunity to elect the same leading power restored....We must accept the fact that a black man is a symbol of poverty, mental deficiency, jealousy, poverty and failure to rule his emotions. A black man is willing to do whatever they can to fend his folly. Give them (African) money for development. They will fight among themselves and cause hostility. Discover oil on their land, they slot themselves mercilessly, and there will be no peace again, for all the days of their lives " ...end of quotes.

Trump in his message expressed obvious prejudice suffered by whites against blacks, but with the racist nature continue to be in their hearts; does not remove the truth about his true mission against us. Why should I send before the words of this message? If you live in

poverty you have twice as reflection is probably due to the characteristics of us black people or other sources, or is it a mental deficiency as Trump wants this matter to Africans explained?.

Before being saved and become the Servant of God, truly I can't lie all the things he talked by the Trump was definitely on my life. We Africans, we should rhetorical and reflect why we remain poor, while we have all the resources that God has given us. Through experience, I met the burden of seeing someone have hatred for the other fellow because he led the examination. Although my family has not done enough to superstition; secured my ability mentally I has at school, but I believe it to other parents with their children and have the mental capacity at the school; they had to go to witchdoctors to witch their children.

That's superstition mentioned by President of the United States, it is true and has been an obstacle to African development.

In life I've been through, nothing that I went through and perform as a heretic intervene, but yet it is only wizards of your progress. I pass through the work of the press, for some time but, when I wrote articles and stories in magazines, I was very disappointed with those around me. When I was employed in several companies the same character of intrigue, nuts, envy, and jealousy continued. We blacks sometimes have the sights and negative thoughts that hinder our own progress.

Africans still thinks prosperities comes by associating with magic, and still thinking development comes from complaining and keeping idle without work and when employed think that without corruption development never come. I used to think and reflect the commitment in the form of liberation from poverty. I thought very much longer, and finally get a new idea, as I came to think, I founded a new thing on earth could rise economically; Then I asked God to help me find a new idea which will making inroads in the world and will put

my life super.

All these thoughts were coming to me because I dislike poverty and I hated even today. God says everyone who asks receives truly as I do . one day in my activities I putted more efforts of researching the science of sports later I discover a variety of new game in this world that does not exist anywhere. When I got this an idea I started immediately to wrote down legislation and later prepared a place for youth to demonstrate the game, it comes popular and attract them and then I decided to take it to the government; be accepted and later sent to schools began to be played and loved so much and then I get in registration.

You know why I explained this is to giving the fact of that message we read from abroad, means that up today I still failed to advance from the intrigues of this blacks.

Everyone tries to pull down your efforts and even

those you follow in order to help you to develop your ideas are not ready because they focus that you're going to get beneficial and your family, so they will try their level best to stop your dream, these are blacks. Even if there are this obstacles am still striving and am sure one day my success will come true.

I speak these words to show you that although Trump massage is intense and bitter to Africans, but I believe Africans cannot forget it for decades, if they have a good sense. While in this massage there many insult but partly filled with facts. Life outside salvation it looks like that , the discord and strife with drunkenness and other pleasures, but the time I saved the pursuit of poverty and hatred for my good fortune that God chosen me to be pastor to his work. I want to tell you that Trump has said the truth, that we are making love or devotion to things of worship but in fact most of it is fiction and we do not know what we do.

I founded a church a certain place here in Africa. When a church got growth within three years, one

pastor came to me and asking if I can accept him to join in my ministries. This was done and made him my assistant, after a few months I left him to go somewhere else to plant another branch, when I left what he did God knows. In few weeks our church members, some of them, were changed has been a heretic and finally the church was torn in two pieces. So then how can I not to believe the words of Trump?

The goal of this chapter, not prescribe the path I took, but I want to reveal and possibly to agree with that; if we choose to reject poverty, we must begin to live as described above. President Trump has fail to restraining his feelings about blacks as he described on thinking for an African says: - "(blacks and Arabs) nothing they have in thinking more than shouting, love music, polygamy, alcohol, superstition, sex uselessly, pretend they love devotion, jealousy, strife, and complained of poor leadership, but do not take any steps to eliminate the worst administration in power.

We must accept the fact that a black man is a "These

words although it is bitter to swallow but if you measured on the sight of truth it is true, but if you really have redeemed logically we must change, we no longer marked as relative poverty as he mentioned. Though, Africa is not society that failed to dominate their feelings, no longer people who have mental deficiency, now days blacks changed totally, there innocent people who cannot use the great force secured ignorance or poverty,. We are no longer slaves to begging, begging is a symptom of laziness . which surprising is when you beg a person who notices that his economy is gained from the environment you are in; then you're not only stupid but foolish.

When I say that, I remember the Bible calls people who turn away from poverty that are not stupid but smart.

We must use any and all weapons to blast the poverty, most of people think that anyone saved should not be rich or have a physical achievement, it is a negative attitude. Thou hast saved is light, we are a model, you deserved to be able to distribute it to the have-

nots. With this work of God still requires you to go forward and give the commitment we have, then we can do the work of evangelization and to reach all nations. I say again and again REJECT POVERTY, shame on you. Look if you mention Jesus, to be your Lord and Savior of your life, then you're in a difficult situation of poverty. Lacking of your need makes some people from being saved, because they wondered; because you are saved and several years gone in salvation but you're in fixed situation up today what will he be saved?

I have tried to read all the sacred texts to see if there are scriptures that show; if any man be saved should be begging or that need food and shelter and wear, not seen anywhere, because everything I read I get an full promise of success in the Lord. What has been a problem then, or is it the Trump explained, or are there other problems? So probably the servant of God does clergy truth? or is it because we are Africans namely

blacks? or ourselves or what then?

One day I went somewhere in a deserted place to meditate about this, after some hours of meditations. I noted in many things are not equal so what I got there satisfied to write all in this little book, but a few I write will extensive knowledge to make you become billionaire in the world. Ideally repeat again to emphasis to say poverty is not part of God's children and should not be so, what exactly is the problem, we asked or we admitted not knowing, who brought us into the same trap we are caught like wildebeest? Truly there is an Answers exist in this book and we must see in this little book of knowledge to bring us a victory.

Most of peoples who I did interview, many of them yearn to leave poverty and do not want to, but I ask why the poor who, because it's become much, but nearly a majority say have NOT A CAPITAL. And some of them pretended that there brother not assist them, or sending to collages , bereavement and family etc. that's what the real truth that causes someone to be

pitied? Of course we need answers, and if we realize does no longer remain poor !.

CHAPTER THREE.

TYPES OF POVERTY.

Within the scriptures there are four main types of poverty, which are known even in the physical world. Yet there are texts that have shaken the first blacks who received the faith. The confusion was made deliberately by the earliest missionaries to tearing down blacks that someone with wealth will go to Heaven (I have the same view but do not necessarily believe it). Texts like these is that brought confusion about the faith to succeed until today;

"..none serve two masters; for either he will hate the one and love the other; or else he will hold to the one,

and despise the other. You cannot serve God and mammon. For that reason I tell you, do not worry about your life, what you eat or drink what you do not your body, what you will wear? "Matthew 6:24-25. "...,

"..for a godliness with contentment is great gain, for we brought nothing into the world, and we will come to nothing, but if we have food and clothing, we will be content with that. But they that will be rich fall into temptation and a snare, and desires many foolish and hurtful, which drown men in destruction and perdition. For the root of all evil is the love of money, which some coveted after, they have erred from the faith and pierced themselves through with many sorrows. "1 Tim 6: 6-10"

"and said there was one slave rich man who dressed in purple and fine linen, and eat all day luxury, and the poor man named Lazarus, which was laid at his gate, full of sores. And desiring to be fed with the crumbs which fell from the rich man's table; even the dogs came and licked his sores. And when the poor man

died and was carried by the angels into Abraham's bosom. The rich man also died and was buried, and then in hell he lift up his eyes, being in torments, and see Abraham afar off, and Lazarus on his chest. He called out, Abraham,

have mercy on me, Apostle Lazarus to dip the tip of his finger in water and cool my tongue; because I am tormented in this flame. Abraham said, Son, remember that you received your good things in your life, and likewise Lazarus evil things; and now he is there he is comforted and thou art tormented "Luke 16: 19-25

"so every one of you who does not give up all his possessions cannot be my disciple "Luke 14:13.

So even if there are other scripture compared with that I can bear; members probably thinking to have money you cannot get into heaven. Of course people who have been given stewardship of interpreting scripture at the same time, that's the part that did not succeed. They could interpret properly scripture, and

as a result will have to be who we are today. Is it really is because the scripture that we want to defend ourselves in that bush? So let me first look at the perceptions of poverty and its form;

The first type: poor in spirit;

The first type is the Bible recognized poverty of spirit (godliness). The Bible has discussed this poverty as a way of renouncing the world things to seek heavenly things. This is not the poverty of lack of income, food or clothing. Many pious and I would say almost all of them; doing there handicrafts for income support their families and their needs, but more for the churches of God put aside their share in jobs that tend to do. Bible speaks very clearly to these poor souls that

"blessed are the poor in spirit; for the kingdom of heaven. "Matthew 5: 3, Exodus 22:25, Mark 12: 43-44. Lk 6:20.

In the meaning of this poverty is the fearing of God and devoted your whole life to do anything to possess the

world, but yourself have made sacrifices to the Lord with all your religious behave. However, this knowledge is not available to every child of God; because if we had it all to God's work would not worked properly , because who would preside over the other activities ?. That is why the Spirit for the common good has distributed gifts to the body of Christ may be built.

The second type: Poverty of physical disabilities:

The second type of poverty recognized by the scriptures is poverty links, physically impaired, namely those who are supposed to help people who are able to work.

"The Spirit of the Lord is upon me, he has anointed me to preach good news to the poor. He has sent me to proclaim to the captives, and sight to the blind, to release the oppressed "Luke 4:18.

Those who the Lord Jesus is talking about in these terms, it is the poor who are disabled who cannot do

anything. Remember it was the ministry of the apostles of Jesus also. Often people have mention Lazarus to raise and discuss the situation of poverty and wealth on the church. Let me tell you, I want these people to read it properly, they will soon discover that Lazarus was poor as he carried the ingredients brought to the king so that she can make a living.

"He said there was a wealthy slave who was clothed in purple and fine linen and luxury to eat all day, and a poor man named Lazarus," is placed at the door "of his, full of sores. And desiring to be fed with the crumbs which fell from the rich man's table; even the dogs came and licked his sores. And when the poor man died and was carried by the angels into Abraham's bosom. The rich man also died and was buried, and then in hell he lift up his eyes, being in torments, and see Abraham afar off, and Lazarus in his chest. And he cried and said, O, Abraham, have mercy on me, Apostle Lazarus to dip the tip of his finger in water and cool my tongue; because I am tormented in this

flame. Abraham said, Son, remember that you received your good things in your life, and likewise Lazarus evil things; and now he is there he is comforted and thou art tormented "Lk 16: 19-25

Lazarus" is placed at the door, "was carried and placed in the courtyard of the king, even a dog could touch his sores. He disabled that whatever he despised so much, because he was dirty, bathe with abundant lesions. Not only had the poor of that days, and beggar. But we found another man, who sits in front of the temple gates, he was healed by Peter and John.

"Now Peter and John were going up to the temple at prayer,. And the man who was lame from his mother's womb was taken by the people, whom they laid daily at the gate of the temple which is called Beautiful, to ask alms to the people who went into the temple"Acts 3:1-2

The Third type; Lacking of income.

This poverty is appeared where a person is able to work, he has all the ingredients of the body,

surrounded by numerous possibilities that he can use them only, can you truly successful but (with the unfolding situation) rather than be successful he himself becomes poor. This is type which especially bears the content of this book. It is the poverty which we often see here Africa for a higher percentage than any other region, thus we closely see the thoughts of Donald Trump as carry meaning for us.

Do we have a culture of poverty or do not know the meaning of the good life? You met someone have a hundred and six cows, and ten out of your kids no one in his children or relatives completed standard. He slept in the house of straw, no electricity and every day he take a witchdoctor to diagnosis her/his home with children, then always is fan of richest club's number one to wealth Manchester United or Barcelona?.do not we agree these false admit that we were bewitched? '

How can a wizard bewitching the whole country?

Let think out of box if you decide from today to do

anything, any job which you have a percentage to earn money how can you remain poor. Today the door is open to successful, so why do yo continue to be poor even if the old things happened that way ?. I think are the cause, and are especially motivated us and providing answers. It is poverty that we talked about, that even scriptural mention it;

"HE THAT LOVETH PLEASURE SHALL BE POOR, AND LOVETH WINE AND OIL SHALL NOT BE RICH" PROVERBS 21:17.

Such people are the ones who speak in the book that if you have your have a good sense and you have a power to working in the life of this world you cannot be poor, and being poor will counted that are you fool.

The fourth type: Poverty of incidence:

This kind of poverty arises from various events that can be manifested to mankind until causes a person or community to be poor. example; if you live where there

is conflict, areas where there are earthquakes, or invasion of any kind which are beyond the capacity of a person, eg matters as wave climate, in which you can work and cultivate, but the problems of climate brought a result up a poor. this situation, are outside run counter to our book, in that sense; as we continue to read and learn that we are talking to the poverty question concerning the third element of self-imposed poverty, ie the person or community surrounded by all opportunities but you found them surrounded of poor.

CHAPTER FOUR:

Meaning of Income Poverty:

This third type of poverty is the poverty of lack of income. This poverty appeared sane person is able to work, he has all the ingredients of the body, surrounded by various opportunities that, he can use them may be rich; but he himself becomes poor. Especially the poor who bears the content of this book. The holy scriptures are trying talking this poverty of one's own self-imposed

"He who loves pleasure will become poor, and love wine and oil shall not be rich" Proverbs 21:17.

Such people are the ones who speak in the book that if you have your minded and working properly in this world you cannot be poor. However it is advisable to know the real meaning and its interpretation of this poverty. Poverty is derived from narrow power of thinking.

When I say it is the harvest, I mean that all he has one,

has been driven by something done before. All he has is a harvest of what was planted; This means that, if a man riding a little think about issues his prospering and live well, will reap the crop trickles to think that will be his poverty and his family and society around and hoping in him or her. For example someone tells you

"God has called me and told me to quit my job to come to serve"

This thing I have heard for many pastors. This is really God knows you have a family, and to spread his work it needs money to run, and submit it to all nations, he dismissed and your family begins to sleep hungry, children do not go to school, your wife, you arguments and fight every day, is really God, or the voice of another man ?.

This is limited thinking, though not that I refuse that GOD call to serve his people. However there is a need to judge yourself in this wisdom; When we read the

scripture that gives us trouble the slogan of " have heard a calling of God" while your children sleeping hungry every dawning day .. I think is not.

"who is wise and understanding among you? Let him show his works by his good conduct, humility and wisdom. However, ye have bitter envying and strife in your hearts, do not boast and do not lie against the truth. This wisdom is not that which comes down from above, but is earthly, sensual; and the devil. because there envying and strife is, there is confusion and every evil work. But the wisdom from above is pure-again-first is the peace-of gently-prepared to listen to the people, full of mercy and good fruits, without partiality, and without hypocrisy "James 3: 15-17.

Should be realistic in that, because everyone who hear God's voice that he must don't . Results of this envy and fool, it bears income poverty. With this type of poverty traced to think less. Africans we feel a bit but Tanzanians we think very little. The church is not a place for people who cannot think about this life. We

need to figure out the fate of our family life we know absolutely is saved but children should go to school and they need shelter and food. Failure to send them to school is one of the rotten way to be prepared the next day begging.

Never not to do so. Figure out what is the profit very spiritual and physical thinking things are very important. In just given some thought to the servants of God who even today do not want to devote to anything because they are servants of God, but I know there are some of us who all called came and he threw his hook was called, and these hooks are not physical but spiritual. The truth is that being a servant of God is not a criterion of being a burden to the church but to set an example. Scripture makes it clear this matter,

"Brothers, we urge in the name of the Lord Jesus Christ, that ye withdraw yourselves from every brother that walked disorderly, and not after the tradition which he received of us. For you yourselves know how you ought to follow us; because we were not disorderly

among you; nor did we eat food from anyone free; but with toil and hardship, night and day we worked, so as to avoid overwhelming any one of you. Not that we do not have orders, but deliberately do ourselves an example to you, follow us, because even when we were you, this we commanded you, that if any would not work, then, not eat. For we hear that some among you who walk without the order, they do not have their own activities, but are concerned about the affairs of others. So urge them, and warn them in the name of Jesus Christ to work quietly and eat their own food ... ..and if anyone did not keep our word in this epistle, and man, do not talk to him, that he may be ashamed; but on him as an enemy, but warn him as a brother. "2 Thessalonians 3:14.

Other terms of the world say if you don't think to get, obviously you think missing. Brother we must be able to think good and evil not to succumb to the same thoughtless, these texts convinces us so let us think how to free themselves from poverty.

POVERTY IS THE CONSEQUENCES OF MIND SLEPT IN THE WORLD OF SPIRIT.

It is true there are BROTHERS with mind lying on, which is not yet wake up and does not know what time it is and what the timing of the rise and autonomy. But if lying is blowing scriptural shouted,

"Wherefore he saith, Awake thou that sleepest, and arise from the dead, and Christ will shine. So watch carefully how you walk, not as unwise but as with wisdom; Redeeming the time, because the days are evil. "Ephesians 5:14:16

MUST not sleep deprivation if we do so reap poverty and as likely as not mind our renown because we can recognize that the mind is probably locked in the spiritual world; so we have delivered otherwise we will live a very difficult life. One scholar and author of books with global service and specialization of knowledge of the winds, brother Jim Murphy (American Missionary) in his book entitled sold and bought too much how to

defeat Demons; makes it clear that, especially the western concepts they disagreed on the idea if there are spirits (demons) can cause a person to be poor and destitute.

He has written the p 25 "unfortunately more, many of our doctrines of the Christian faith on the winds built on the foundations of set by the fathers of the spotlight than that on the (basis of the apostolic and prophetic) Eph 2:20. We the West we hold culture occurring prefer logic and reason giving, rather than who can be known only by the spirit and emotions. Things have been intellectual than spiritual. "Logic" rule; "**Spiritual feeling**" treasure weight "This knowledge is sometimes routed through colleges of Theology and enter with us in developing countries to start seriously ignore the required discovery to this type of obstacle to church and people seeking development. Pp 21-28.

Located mainly examples in our country of Tanzania we can Consecration example, it is not surprising that and you may find one is busy or is employed and has a

good salary, but it is poor, it does nothing!. Such a person must self-assessment in these areas is what !? His mind is asleep or demonic? Some people think that if you be saved can no longer escape persecution by demons, you are fooling yourself, if it is so then why apostle Paul he failed to make some of its operations because it was prevented by a messenger of the devil.

"So we wanted to come to you, even I Paul, the first time and again, and Satan hindered us"

You can have good plans but Satan interfered with your schedule and make it tough. In the example of the apostle Paul, you know what I have described here. Not that the apostle was not saved, was clean again full of the Holy Spirit, but met with the same persecution, how you and me!?. It is possible you do not be a demon in you, but the demon said to go ahead, enter into other people you want to associate with the common business, and eventually all of the capital loan is unable to return to your home sold and remains poverty. Also Satan can deceive you even if

you are saved. Ananias is our class field, because we see Peter saying,

"Peter said, Ananias, why hath Satan filled your heart to lie to the Holy Spirit and to keep back part of the price of the land? "

Ananias was born-again clean and godly, but met with this issue of being deceived. There are many types and demons of different functions that can shackle your minds became you think the opposite; and agree to erroneous ideas, and at the same time you feel you're right and yet it is only capable of demonic.

POVERTY IS LAZY AND IMPOSED FALIER DISTINGUISH RIGHT FROM WRONG.

IT IS CLEAR known that if a person lazy and can not work it must be poor. This is why one should be careless and lazy? Before you know too much about this is we know better what is negligence and laziness is. Negligence is the one to reach the state of his career, but he made without productivity; ie he did the

work that sluggish, half-hour work is done in three hours. And lazy is the state's failure to ACT ANYTHING. He cannot go to the field or factory, loves to sleep or talk too much at the same location. Lazy not get up early, winter is a coward; and everything to do to him is heavy, it is often a refinancing matters. Now we want to answer our question why a person that is lazy or careless means many reasons but the main reason is BAD SENSE, and failure to control the feelings, corresponding to a negative feature. Holiest of All Scripture clearly highlighted, that loves sleep will be poor.

INCOME IS POVERTY HAS NO SIGNS THAT THE HOLY SPIRIT.

I know this may bring much debate about the Holy Spirit and poverty. But if you pursue it properly you will discover is the same, These shall be of the Holy Spirit and the same time you are lazy or careless or do not want to work? The Holy Spirit is our guide in all good. Is laziness and incompetence are all good, who

can refer you to GUIDE you pleasing to God? NOT rhetorical refusal before as there correctly or not. So even if we admit that whomsoever; then you will be very grieved when Scripture says do not grieve the Holy Spirit who dwells in you. CHECK Holy Spirit in you wants to strengthen

"But ye shall receive power, when he had come upon you the Holy Spirit, and you shall be my witnesses" Acts 1: 8 ...... compare this verse **"But remember the Lord; He is your God gives you power to get wealth "Deuteronomy 8:18.**

This is a hard swallow it, but it's the truth; in the Holy Spirit you can self-awareness and self-knowledge of your situation in life you have. Within the Holy Spirit, who you claim you're him, but your children are begging on the street what might this matter? He is a devout one never write texts which have no doubt about it, that is scriptural

"I have been young, and now am old; yet have I not

seen the righteous forsaken, nor his seed begging bread" Psalm 37:25.

These words show the truth of this be true if you have a Holy Spirit will help that it must work to help you increase your income or provide you with an income.

POVERTY IS PSYCHIC BONDS OF FAMILY.

If there is poverty that has ruled some countries then it can become its main source comes from this aspect of the psychic bonds of family and clan or tribe. This kind of poverty is difficult to discover and accept the deal with them, because you have hid themselves in the consciousness of people. Many Christians are saved before they were born and raised in a repressive African traditions that are not completely aware of the issues and the economic success, science, and technology.

Many were born under the leadership and governance of the spirits of family and clan. For this one has to be saved one comes not. Know yourself or meet and

proper pastor who know what I have stated to be made meaningful DELIVERANCE, aimed at eliminating poverty mark on the person. But amazingly you can escape for the pastor whom he remains bound this area, so Do not expect to get change can happen. Writes IYKE NATHAN OZORMA, Ph.D in his book KNOW YOUR ENEMY, BE CAREFUL WITH FRIENDS. PG 65 on the poverty of the psychic, cites that;

There were a businessman whose business was unsellable. This man came to seek the help of God. He has had products from China to sell in Nigeria all impaired, -no one had bought. These products were worth roughly twelve million naira. The money was used to buy these products had loaned from bank. When he came, I took time to pray, meditate and seek the face of the Holy Spirit about the source of his problem. The spiritual message given to me is that his business block came with his wife .... in spirit I saw his wife, who was sleeping and change to be ants .. "

In the spiritual world you might have ghosts that bring poverty through yourself or your wife, or someone working with him on business . Ghosts exist and should be addressed is where things can be clarified. Most Christians are the church members and are poor, but not that they would to have the poor, but all they are doing is dying so to win this circumstances and attitudes fighting to offer, but as a result it becomes nothing. I grew up in intellectual family which at that time was prosper family, and it was remote but it was with the greatest potential financial issues. In my eyes I was still a child, I saw my uncles were dug in the kitchen bury millions of money it was excessive. Our grandmother was looking after us was unused all, without having to use specialized storage.

But as right now I wrote this book, this family is very poor. the house was built with stone carved but now is like house of madness. These rich uncles, have died in a shameful. Surely the ghosts cut off family in in front the eyes of us. what happened in our family to this

point I have described. Ghosts are destroyed totally life of the family and they would not ask to God may this chain of poverty continued to pursue the family.

That father of the spirits of his wife in Nigeria came close to completely liquidating as the submitted to God. Much poverty we have today among us is due to these spirits of clan and family. With this knowledge, you'll need to test yourself know the situation arises and what you're going through, does not have the knowledge or capital or what then?

POVERTY IS THE RESULT OF APATHY, IGNORANCE AND SQUANDERED.

But there is also this poverty of ignorance, ie poverty sensuality that could have been avoided. Careless your income, no income and expenditure register this it is another pub that ridiculous compulsion. And strangely, even what little available. For, to succeed be required what goes into and what comes be much less. then they can see the benefit of you did work. But you find

one, not any rules but their use has been very high and do not fear nor worry. We all know that the property would be lost without notebook.

POVERTY OF RELATIONSHIPS.

There is some kind of poverty that happens to someone from the relationships that they have with someone, perhaps your wife; or who meet in her husband, or even a relative who is working with you on doing business or working with him. Relationships are very important, because without knowing in detail the relationships you entered; can cost you in the future. Example those boys who love to sleep sexually disposal and girls, there are many failures in life percent, due to the misfortune will come upon those gathered for the women who met with all sorts of men.

One of the weapons to succeed is to leave adultery or fornication meant sleeping with a prostitute is united with him, and that one body so as to ghosts and spirits of poverty will leave it, you do it all operations must and

will die alone. That is why God forbids adultery in part to keep us out of the ghostly connections. Even those who depend on the issue of sexual devil observed so that anyone can succeed.

Within relationships we need very seriously and there should know each other, if not so you will lost all; For the owner to have it is to be poor spirits without him knowing. Author UZORMA says you should know exactly hostile but you're on multiple intelligence measure should keep friends, this thing I trusted to be true. There are ones they were developed before marrying, but after marrying, their capitals turned back until they go bankrupt. If someone had observer would notice that the woman who marries has a problem, let deal with that before putting money back into the business.

POVERTY OF ALTAR:

I have decided to use the word because of ritual altar ritual done a certain area psychic. There will likely be a

poor man from the area he is. There are some areas that are not safe to live or conduct business because the area is not safe for a successful and uplifting. Topped locations in a country or borders of a country or region cannot perform activities moving well, either until the bike or break and demolish the previous authority of Satan to the power of Jesus' name. But because you do not know you have just made, and the result becomes a loss. We have seen many times in the scriptures such things, safe place and elsewhere are not marked. This included access to capital which is derived from the blood of people or you come directly to the altar of the devil.

If you do not know where that capital came from is really doing business but eventually you earn nothing . In the area of poverty of altars there are altars demonic in some churches of Christian that you find church's taught that all the money you will get to take it first to that altar for pray for. sometimes have the teaching of resist money, saying money is the devil.

So while on the altar like this you do not get successful because the spirits present on the altar.

CHAPTER FIVE.

claimant.

Shall be finalized if all the problems that have gone on to explain that in the last frame then there is that if we view the cause we will not see anyone complain about poverty. In my research I pass through various interviews with various people and I realized that almost many excluding minor defects, complain that they do not have capital.

To many it was believed claiming they only get money for capital can be rich. Here let me ask you, that African countries are poor because they have no capital? Does it really matter? If so let ask our Government, has everything a mining model does not ?, Parks does not ?, Sea and port do capitalized? Why now are still considered a poor country. Of course there is something which causes to fail, and here we want to learn together that, claiming, the issue of

saying you do not have a capital delete it from today in your head and now began to regroup in order to open the door of success from now on.

Given the thirst I had to succeed, and that was in my power to the questions that is why I am poor, Lord had opened a door of secret knowledge I know why I'm still so, and if I want to succeed then I have to monitor several things as I will list it here.

THERE ARE FIVE capitals we could use which some would not even have a single penny in hand and eventually millions began to enter into his account without having any worries. If you saved a very insufficient, and you will succeed quickly but if not saved will succeed as a second after the first successful who are the devout. But before I bring this knowledge would let you know that: It is dangerous for anyone who wants to succeed, if you stay with ought working twenty-four hours, with ought getting five hundred shillings per day. It becomes more dangerous because the time that you were in that situation , you

took your own five hundred from your account, and submit to the nets that ensnare others. You need to be shrewd in getting success, make sure you have the ENTER-NET.

RULE ONE: Fear God.

The first principle of success and the economic rise should be devout every called today. This is the principle lightweight hard again, will depend on your willingness; if you like and you'd to serve God. This principle is accepted all over the world and they have almost all economies except scientists. According to the bible scriptures reads,

" acquaint now yourself with him and be at peace ; thereby good shall come unto thee" Job 22:21.

this will help you remove the edges that can be draw on you like bad luck, curses, demons, disapproval etc.

PRINCIPLE TWO: have knowledge.

The second principle, it must have the knowledge, the search for knowledge and be aware of the various items will help increase your early even if there was none like cash, eg if you would know how to speak English fluently you invited to address interpret and would be paid with ought capitalized money.

I have my fellow friend Pastor make laughing when we had a Bible college. When we were discussing some issues talking about the importance of knowing more languages of Swahili; the pastor can help make his pastoral work effectively. He told that there when the Europeans came to his church for to help,. Since he did not know English went looking for a man who has not saved so should introduce as elder be his interpreter. The whites had a meeting with that interpreter, and after the meeting, the man went on to get an opportunity to talk to them. After some time passed waiting white shepherd to accomplish their promises at that that man was never seen again and

the village was retrieve information later is that the man was invited and went to Sweden for the whites and that promise to church till today did not occur.

PRINCIPLE THREE: realize your potentials.

There are potentials that are the main capital which God putted into a man. For the this is equivalent to saying grace given to human achievement that his life force to organize one's standards. These potentials are a variety of places that I believe if someone calm down and understand its value it can help him to go further.

This is what we call the capital of the divine that if you choose to use it you cannot become a poor;

LIFE:

Did you wake up with a life? you have your health? ... if you find you wake up you have whole and healthy, it is your capital realized you could make get anything you want. Use this life income.

POWER:

Did you wake up with a full strength? If you feel you awake to life and no longer have the force that is clearly recognized that you can use it to make the investments in the power to earn money. You must know how to use the power given in order to earn a living. Power is bringing wealth. Deuteronomy 8:18

GOOD MIND:

I used to think so, the mind of man has the same size as the borders of his country. My idea is that produced a question like that, then I am having spent much part of the mind so that I can redeem the difficult situation I had. The answer I found was that I laughed, because I feel I think even beyond the borders of our village where I was born. What if I think the breadth of the county, or divisions, or district or region will have to do what standards ?. Brothers given to us to take the mind to finish this disease of poverty. Wealth and success exist and you are waiting for you, except, do you have

the sense to recognize it? If you have a sound mind to use it properly and you know you will not die poor.

TALENTS :

I may wonder if you have a talent or skill and then you say I do not have capital. For what is my capital? Tell you !? Right now as you read this my book, ready for my brilliant I earn money because having the gift of writing, do you have the skills; what would you say no money; . Go America, go to Russia, go to many developed countries, so the talent and skills of the people running the latest life. Wealth is in the talent you have, and possess skills Trouble is your mind know how to do. No one can steal your talent or skill of one person, except the ignorance that is in one of the ones you can be its own enemy.

OPPORTUNITIES:

In life you live and you're in you ever seen opportunities ?. I want to tell you all within an hour must be no more than two opportunities you can use

that day income. You must be a student to identify opportunities, opportunity is money and opportunity is life,

FAITH:

Faith is one of the placements in you what is important and you should have it; and to learn in order to succeed in your life movement. Faith is a spiritual weapon that works great in your activities. Faith is the engine of success, everything that you see in this world, and developed a lot of what you see in this world have come to trust. This thing is absolutely certain because God Almighty himself tells us that even the world itself was created by faith. You can read the eleventh chapter of the book of Hebrews, then you'll know

absolutely that faith is the very meaning placements within. Succeed or initiate any project must have faith, and without faith you can not please God and neither can succeed and accomplish your goals.

PRINCIPLE FOUR: IMPLIMANTATION:

It must go through all the rules for the layout can succeed easily, and propose the optimal regulation Disagree fly because every action has its victories degrees of success. This principle of four touches all implementing

regulations, so if you skip one regulations are intended Do not access your destiny. Broadly speaking if you still feel you're alive realize your destiny to succeed is in place. Now let look own implementation of this principle in the fourth. Here are five things that are necessary in the implementation regulations.

PLAN:

If you want success you must have a special program AND PLAN that can remind you to move in good direction. Plan carries all your vision you have.

OBJECTIVE:

Your program must comply with the objectives that

show how your program can be effectively accomplished.

DARE:

If you set your goals and see have gone properly, must believe in daring to implementation process.

SACRIFICE:

Again we must sacrifice, gaining success is not a game we must sacrifice indeed amount of risk your life. Remember this one thing, that going to heaven is too difficult, than there is easier to make money. Now if you cannot find the money to how to heaven?

ENDURE:

Discover this and be careful with it. You cannot succeed with ought patient. Endure is a pleasure to be able to battle the enemy poverty must endure before quitting or complaining.

PRINCIPAL FIVE;

ETHICS.

I'm confident that you can succeed and no long you will not be the former who was despised. Now there is much to consider in this final code of ethics:

PRESERVE TIME:

It is advisable to be discovered to keep the time . Realize you have eight hours of rest, eight hours of work and eight hours of slumber. I used it because I would work 12 hours to rest and work 4 to 8 to sleep.

CONTROL EMOTIONS:

Many people have failed to dominate their emotions make them at this time of their lives. It must be able to rule your heart and your body and your soul as well. If you do not dominate your feelings you cannot afford to pay to achieve the goals you set. Learn to be faithful in your affairs.

HAVE AN ACCOUNTS.

YOU HAVE home bank. If you NEED to have success you braid programs must sign up cord immediately bought mute put your house ready to preserve your money,

CHAPTER SIX.

MAIN PRINCIPLE TO BECOME RICH

Most people, if not all of us, want to live in financial comfort and stability. We want to be rich, to be able to buy anything we want, and to have access to a premium lifestyle. While the end goal is clear, it's hard to know where to begin your journey to being wealthy.

Before you get started, it's important to acknowledge that becoming rich takes time and effort. There are very few ways to instantly have large amounts of wealth, and all of them are luck-based. Not all of us can win the lottery or inherit a fortune from a mysterious rich relative. Becoming rich in most cases involves a lot of hard work, patience, and time. There are some tried-and-true things you can do that can help you get rich, but the key is to constantly and consistently work hard, keep track of yours and keep your eyes on the prize.

1. Add Value

Something many self-made wealthy people have in common is that they are valuable in specific ways. Even when millionaires and billionaires are taken out of the equation, many rich people — doctors, engineers, filmmakers — have gotten rich after adding value to themselves and then adding value to the world. For example, a rich neurosurgeon may be specially talented and skilled. This surgeon added value to the world after improving their own skills and quality of life.

Adding value to yourself is a good foundation to begin your journey to being rich. Develop some knowledge or skills that justify someone paying you a good amount of money. Convince people that you are worth a large paycheck because you will add value to their lives in return.

1. Tax Yourself

The concept of saving money is not a new one. However, it is extremely easy to "dip into your savings"

when you want something badly enough. The key to accomplishing your goal of amassing wealth is to actually try and save money.

A different way of looking at your savings is to view them as taxes. Once you pay your taxes, you never get the whole amount back. Treat your savings the same way. Set money aside in a savings account or transfer it to a totally separate account where you cannot touch it. Treat your savings like money that you will never get back, until the day that you get it all back at once.

3. Create a Plan and Follow It

The likelihood of suddenly stumbling upon unlimited riches is extremely low. While it may seem that a lot of the success stories you hear are luck-based, this is actually not true. There is probably some chance and luck involved, but most rich people became rich through meticulous planning and discipline.

This includes things like budgets and timelines, as well as a plan of what to do at every step of the way to

success. It is important not to get complacent and do your best to keep going, and having a plan helps without wasting unnecessary amounts of time. Creating a budget and following it is only one part of this process.

4. Invest

The core principle behind investing is that you end up making more money than you spent. However, it is important to choose your investments wisely. There are plenty of places for you to sink your money into, but figuring out which one of these will result in you profiting is difficult.

Real estate is sometimes a good investment, but it is expensive. Investing in the stock market does not have to be expensive, but it can be risky and unstable. A 401K is a wise investment that you should invest in, but it can depend on how well the business you work for is doing. There are plenty of factors to consider when investing, so make sure you think about it rationally.

Talk to experts or friends who are experienced in investing before making a decision.

5. Start a Business

This is much easier said than done, but the last four steps lay the groundwork to be able to start your own business. If you have a knack for business or want to be your own boss, this can be a great step to making some money. However, as many entrepreneurs will tell you, creating your own business requires massive upfront costs and low revenue in the beginning.

Being an entrepreneur is not a quick way to get rich — it is a massive change in lifestyle. It has its unique trials and rewards, and in many cases is totally worth it. However, this is not a choice to be taken lightly. It requires commitment, grit, and some luck to be successful. While it may take some time, it can certainly help you get wealthy.

6. Be Grateful

Becoming rich does not only require external factors to fall into place — many personality factors have to align for you to succeed at whatever venture you've started. Staying humble and grateful for the progress you've made at every step of the way is essential.

People do not want to give their money to someone who does not appear to appreciate it, or gets too carried away with any moderate amount of success. Keeping your life in perspective and having a considerate, thankful, and humble attitude is the way to go.

7. Develop Patience

Another important personality trait to being successful and rich is patience. Nothing big is accomplished overnight, and you cannot and will not get rich in a matter of days. All the efforts you put towards accumulating wealth could take months or even years

to pay off. It's easy to get frustrated early on, especially when it seems like there's a new wealthy person in the news every other day. However, realizing that your pace of success does not have to compete with theirs is crucial.

In the long run, patience can be extremely rewarding. This does not mean that you should get complacent or wait things out instead of taking risks. Success can take some time, and getting frustrated is detrimental to your efforts.

8. Educate Yourself

It is key to try and educate yourself, not only in your chosen field but also in the ways of the world. Keeping up with the news, for example, is extremely important if you want to make a decision about investing or find out about upcoming trends. Ignorance is the prime killer of any efforts to make money.

This means you have to constantly educate yourself. You cannot let major events or trends slide, because in

each of them there is a threat or opportunity for you. Staying aware and educating yourself about current events is essential.

9. Take Calculated Risks

There is no money made without a risk taken. Whether it's starting a business or investing in stocks, every avenue to making money requires some risk. Even selling your old furniture requires you taking the risk that the buyer will show up and will pay you. It is a comparatively small risk when compared to deciding whether to spend millions of dollars on a new product line, but it is still a risk.

In order to make money, you have to take a chance that a venture or idea you have will pan out. Therefore, it is important to think deeply and evaluate multiple possible outcomes before you decide that an investment is worth it. Taking risks without thinking about them beforehand is an incredibly quick way to lose money. To earn, you should take risks, but they

should be calculated.

10. Give Back

It is important to give back to the community. This leads back to the first point about adding value to the world around you. If you earn some money, give some back to a cause you believe in. This way, you are adding value to the world after having added value to yourself.

Another benefit of giving to charity is that people perceive you as a better person when you give to causes they care about. They are likely to trust you more when they see that you aren't intent on hoarding the money they give you, and that doing so will benefit their community in turn. Of course, the tax benefits of giving to charity are also a great incentive to do so.

Being rich means something different to every individual. Some people are happy with a decent-sized home and a moderate-income job, while others want to be millionaires and billionaires. Regardless of where

you feel you fall on the spectrum, these steps can help you achieve the level of wealth you want. Before you get started, though, make sure to sort out your so your bank account is ready to expand.

May God blessed you

ABOUT ARTHOR.

Edwin karokola is a senior pastor married with five children. He is hold advanced diploma in theological college.

ABOUT BOOK.

Did you know that to be a poor it is too complicated matter, than to become a rich!? It is only a few techniques you never knew, so if you know it, do you no longer become a poor again!!

The book gives you all the secrets, make your colleagues rich, why don't you!? It does not matter WHAT circumstances you are in, it just to determine to dare.

DIE POOR!? Yes/no!!

DIE POOR!?

Yes/no!!

Edwin karokola